YOUR KNOWLEDGE HAS VALUE

- We will publish your bachelor's and master's thesis, essays and papers

- Your own eBook and book - sold worldwide in all relevant shops

- Earn money with each sale

Upload your text at www.GRIN.com
and publish for free

Arghya Ray

Social Shaping Theory as a Derivative of Technological Determinism

GRIN Verlag

Bibliografische Information der Deutschen Nationalbibliothek:

Die Deutsche Bibliothek verzeichnet diese Publikation in der Deutschen Nationalbibliografie; detaillierte bibliografische Daten sind im Internet über http://dnb.d-nb.de/ abrufbar.

Dieses Werk sowie alle darin enthaltenen einzelnen Beiträge und Abbildungen sind urheberrechtlich geschützt. Jede Verwertung, die nicht ausdrücklich vom Urheberrechtsschutz zugelassen ist, bedarf der vorherigen Zustimmung des Verlages. Das gilt insbesondere für Vervielfältigungen, Bearbeitungen, Übersetzungen, Mikroverfilmungen, Auswertungen durch Datenbanken und für die Einspeicherung und Verarbeitung in elektronische Systeme. Alle Rechte, auch die des auszugsweisen Nachdrucks, der fotomechanischen Wiedergabe (einschließlich Mikrokopie) sowie der Auswertung durch Datenbanken oder ähnliche Einrichtungen, vorbehalten.

Imprint:

Copyright © 2010 GRIN Verlag GmbH
Druck und Bindung: Books on Demand GmbH, Norderstedt Germany
ISBN: 978-3-656-57569-6

This book at GRIN:

http://www.grin.com/en/e-book/232792/social-shaping-theory-as-a-derivative-of-technological-determinism

GRIN - Your knowledge has value

Der GRIN Verlag publiziert seit 1998 wissenschaftliche Arbeiten von Studenten, Hochschullehrern und anderen Akademikern als eBook und gedrucktes Buch. Die Verlagswebsite www.grin.com ist die ideale Plattform zur Veröffentlichung von Hausarbeiten, Abschlussarbeiten, wissenschaftlichen Aufsätzen, Dissertationen und Fachbüchern.

Visit us on the internet:

http://www.grin.com/

http://www.facebook.com/grincom

http://www.twitter.com/grin_com

Social Shaping Theory as a Derivative of Technological Determinism

By

Arghya Ray

Introduction

Technological determinism or TD can be described as a reductionist framework that can be used to explore the interrelations between humans and scientific technologies. However, several scholars like Dosi (1982) preferred to develop a broader perspective on technological determinism on the basis of more intricate analysis of technology change and innovation management. According to the scholars like Mackenzie and Wajcman (1999), a major drawback of technological determinism is its rigidity which is resulted by the deterministic nature of this theory. Such an approach, as advocated by its early proponents like Thorstein Veblen, restricts is suppleness to explain the complex attributes of different social processes especially in relationship with innovation management (Tilman 2004).

Essay question

Discuss social shaping theory as an offshoot of technological determinism.

What is social shaping theory?

In order to understand the social shaping theory, a researcher must explore the works of Mackenzie and Wajcman (1985). The authors, in fact, pioneered the concept of social shaping as put in an organised way in their research on the basis of historical analysis. Earlier, scholars like Dosi (1982) had tried to draw attention of the academic world towards influence of society on technology. Dosi (1982) marked technological developments of almost all categories as consequences of an intricate interplay between different economical and institutional factors in the human society as a whole. Although this practically turns technological determinism almost upside down, inclusion of institutional factors remains quite practical and necessary in the context of giant corporations and capitalist democracies. As put forward by the experts like Williamson (1975) and Mackenzie and Wajcman (1985), corporations approach plays an important role to investigate the function of the different corporate institutions behind financing the various support mechanisms for technological research.

Mackenzie and Wajcman (1985) not only focussed on corporations approach, but also utilised many other techniques to find out what factors can affect or lead to a technology change. Researchers like Adler (2006) think that this is like an attempt to understand technological determinism from a broader perspective. Indeed, social shaping theory (Mackenzie and Wajcman 1999) is based on the concept that there are various options which can be explored in designing a technological artefact or system; and the trajectory of research and development programmes in this direction depend on the way those options are selected. However, the very focus of social shaping theory remains on technological development.

Social shaping theory in relation with technological determinism

Adler (2006) has clearly shown that how technology determinism (TD) is related to social shaping theory and vice versa. According to Adler (2006, paragraph 4),

> "As concerns technology's causes, one form of soft TD allows that social factors may shape technology even though, once shaped, technology's effects are (weakly or strongly) determinate; hard TD argues that social influences have little effect on the nature of technology; anti-TD views highlight the social forces that shape the design and development of technology."

Nevertheless, a hardliner technological determinist cannot find any relationship between the two doctrines. According to the tenets of hard technology determinism, only technology is the determining factor in social functionary. Future of a technology is determined on the basis of the experience with its predecessor technologies. For example, research to develop better versions of a certain kind of agricultural fertilizer will be financed if and only if industry experience with the existing fertilizer is positive.

At this level, the tendencies that aim at justifying technological determinism in its most extreme and orthodox form are much based on the deterministic nature of this theory. In fact, the detrimental effects of excessive determinism have been diagnosed in several theories regarding social change. For example, Bottommore (1972, pp. 74-76) has cautioned the academic world about the concept of "economic determinism" since it aims to give an absolute explanation of all social processes on the basis of the doctrine that economy is most important in human civilisation.

However, with the development of the softer versions of technological determinism, powerful argument in favour of a combination of social and technological factors emerges. This argument can be used for explaining innovation and technology change. Scholar's like Tilman (2004) have now raised the question that how the proponents of technological determinism would actually react if they were presented with a softer version the theory. Adler (2006) also appears to be in favour of a softer version of TD. According to him, social factors do play an important role in shaping the technology. Also, the effects of a technology depend on the dynamics of the social environment within which it is developed and used. Social context actually encourages or discourages the use of a technology and the related processes such as research and development. That is why even most conventional and useful technologies may be phased out with the lapse of time and new tools and techniques are adopted despite of initial unfamiliarity and other difficulties (Bottommore 1972; Verma 1968). Therefore, if TD is explained from a softer and suppler perspective it can give rise to the basic postulates of social shaping theory as explained by Mackenzie and Wajcman (1999 and 1985).

Conclusion

Although the social shaping theory cannot be regarded as a direct consequence of technological determinism, the softer versions of the latter can be used to deduce the former. Conversely, flexible interpretation TD can give rise to thoughtful considerations regarding the social context of technology. If technology can shape the course of social development, society can also shape the course of technological development until and unless some major breakthrough or upheaval takes place. So it can be stated without fear of contradiction that technological deterministic concepts can be used to enrich and empower social shaping theory all the more.

List of References

Adler P.S. (2006), Technological determinism. In. S. Clegg and J.R. Bailey (Eds.), *International Encyclopedia of Organization Studies*, New Delhi and Thousand Oaks: SAGE

Bottommore, T.B. (1972), *Sociology: A Guide to Problems and Literature*, Mumbai: George Allen and Union

Dosi, G. (1982), Technological paradigms and technological trajectories: A suggested interpretation of the determinants and directions of technical change, *Research Policy*, 11, 147-162

MacKenzie, D. and Wajcman, J. (1999), *The Social Shaping of Technology*. Buckingham: Open University Press

MacKenzie, D., and Wajcman, J. (Eds.) (1985), *The Social Shaping of Technology: How the Refrigerator got its Hum*, Milton Keynes: Open University Press.

Tilman, R. (2004), *Thorstein Veblen, John Dewey, C. Wright Mills and the Generic Ends of Life*, Oxford: Rowman and Littlefield

Verma, P. (1968), Technological Change and Industrial Organisation: The British Case. *Indian Journal of Industrial Relations*, 4, pp. 186-198.

Williamson, O. (1975), *Markets and Hierarchies: Analysis and Antitrust Implications*, New York: Free Press